MW00451124

STRENGTHS LIFE: UPGRADED

Take Your StrengthsFinder/CliftonStrengths Results to the Next Level

VOLUME FOUR

Using Your Strengths to Create the Life of Your Dreams

Copyright © 2019 by Strengths Life and Zach Carlsen

All rights reserved.

Cover & design by Zach Carlsen

Produced in the United States of America

www.ZachCarlsen.com

a cosmic community

45.0560° N, 92.8088° W

Distributed by you, me, word of mouth, & elbow grease

20 19 18 17   5 4 3 2 1

Second Edition

Table of Contents

Section One: Strategic Thinking Strengths Themes

Section Two: Building the Strengths Mindset

SOME OF US THINK HOLDING ON MAKES US STRONG; BUT SOMETIMES IT IS LETTING GO.

HERMANN HESSE

From the Author:

In the last decade, I've shared in thousands of conversations about Strengths. As a coach, it has been my mission to explore with my clients each aspect of what it means to be Strengths focused and to live from a place of "what it possible", instead of "what needs fixing."

What I have found, time and time again, is that when we are each able to get out of our own we can step into a life with greater meaning, less stress, and more aliveness. There is no greater tool that I have found than StrengthsFinder/ CliftonStrengths to begin this journey to personal freedom.

The following pages are organized into two distinct sections. The first is a deep dive into one of the four Strengths Domains, which are: Executing, Influencing, Strategic Thinking, and Relationship Building. These are categories designed by the creators of the StrengthsFinder/ CliftonStrengths, which organizes the 34 Strengths Themes into specific clusters.

The Strengths Themes represented in this collection are in the Strategic Thinking Domain—Analytical, Context, Futuristic, Ideation, Input, Intellection, Learner, and Strategic.

The second section of this book includes a collection of observations and reflections about how a "Strengths mindset" can best develop in each of us. This section is based on the epic coaching conversations I've had with people all over the world about their Strengths and the countless of hours of study and writing on this powerful tool.

The idea in both sections is to expand on the base that has created by Strengths ambassadors around the globe and the idea here is to explore each theme more deeply than ever. The idea is not to challenge the already established ideas regarding each of the 34 Strengths Themes. Instead, in the following pages, those original ideas will be built upon and, in some cases, unpacked more thoroughly than what is presently available online and in print.

I know of no more effective tool than StrengthsFinder/CliftonStrengths for creating awareness around team dynamics and understanding the core of what drives each of us individually. Playing to our strengths allows us to become more of who we are, instead of trying to become 'better' at what we are not.

With Gratitude,

Zach—*Ideation, Connectedness, Input, Strategy, Empathy*

SECTION ONE: STRATEGIC THINKING STRENGTHS THEMES

What Is the ANALYTICAL Theme

People with the Analytical theme love data, research, and rational, linear lines of thinking. For them, there is an intrinsic value in the explanation of a concept, the proof. It is their instinct to ask "Why?" and "How do you know?" and "How did we get here?". Even if something seems true or obvious, they still like to know why. And, if there are facts, stats, and figures available—even better. They like to know the details, the whys and the hows, and the tangibles before they accept an idea, a claim, or a position on an issue. They are not afraid to poke at another's thinking, testing its validity and overall soundness. Nor are they afraid to change their own mind if better evidence surfaces for a different viewpoint. For them, it isn't rude to challenge someone else's thinking because they are constantly challenging their own thinking. They pride themselves on their objectivity and their ability to remain detached and calm, even in highly charged situations. Theories don't impress them much either. They feel most alive in their thinking when they can be rigorous and unrestrained in their questioning, fact- checking, and research. Their desire for objectivity reveals truths sometimes hidden under layers at the core of our world and our lives.

Why Should We Care

These are the people who are naturally wired to seek answers. They prove/disprove and then explain. And, they do this by asking questions, gathering facts, and doing research. We can count on them to be able to back-up what they are talking about—and they expect the same from others. The latter can draw out the best in us, by encouraging rigor and excellence. People with the Analytical theme are adept at finding patterns as well as the underlying structures of a problem, thought, or situation. They are happy to dig in deep and find out what is or is not working in an idea, scenario, or organization.

Sorting through and synthesizing huge quantities of information, data, and research may be energizing for them. It sets and resets their compass points. From there—from a place of objective clarity—they skillfully structure their ideas, layer them, and formulate bulletproof conclusions.

Ten Things to Know About People with ANALYTICAL

1.   Trust. At their core, what they bring is straightforwardness. Their worldview is, in a sense, provable; it is backed by facts and careful

research. While it can be irksome to some, we can, in the end, trust them—really truly trust them.

2.   Tact. Finding the right words and the appropriate tone is the ongoing work of Analytical folks who, when seeking clarity, can be perceived as unnecessarily critical, dismissive, or rigid.

3.   Outcomes. What they rely on to create their world is that which is provable, and that which can be shared. It may not be enough for them to simply reach a given outcome, they may need to know specifically why the conclusion was such.

4.   Emotion. For someone who is highly Analytical, emotion isn't necessarily viewed as a virtue. The feelings of others as well as their own feelings may, in fact, seem inconvenient, baffling, or slightly problematic for them.

5.   Patterns. They have a knack for patterns and they have a generalized fondness for that which can be repeated, reproduced, and replicated. Things with distinct, identifiable beginnings, middles, and ends have a solid resonance with them.

6.   Spock. They love logic. Don't be surprised if an Analytical person verbally identifies as being "logical". It can be a comfort for them to state it explicitly so that others know.

7.   Intuition. Analytical folks can have the tendency to dismiss that which cannot be quantified—like dreams, the visions of others, and fringe ideas. Their intuition, however, is intact. It manifests as their instinct to test and challenge the world.

8.   Answers. They generally dislike feelings of limbo. It's particularly important for them to determine where they stand on an issue and why. They may go to great lengths researching a topic to avoid feeling or appearing wishy-washy.

9.   Grey. For some, their thinking can appear a bit black and white. That is, things are either all one way or all another. When this is clearly the case, it's okay to ask them why they think or feel that way. Many folks with Analytical actually enjoy being asked to support their ideas and explain them to others.

10.   Love. They may show love and support in nuanced ways. For example, they may feel like they're doing someone a favor by challenging their idea or thinking because it will lead to a stronger, more solid argument. They are also big on acts of service as a way of showing love—something that produces a result.

What Is the CONTEXT Theme

Those with Context are the people in our lives who instinctively look to the past to understand the present. For them, the here and now is simply and concretely the product of what has come before it. In that way, the more information they have about what has been, the more deeply they can appreciate, know, and recognize the present. Looking back is also how they plan for the future. They believe that what we do in each moment is important because it will soon be the past we are looking back on. So, "What happened last time?" can be a sacred question for them. An awareness of the past allows them to honor it, learn from it, and avoid pitfalls. The clearer their understanding of what the "before" was like, the more stable their present moment is. And, consequently, the more confident they will feel about moving ahead. The past, it seems, is perpetually creating the future—and, the now is simply how we get there. People with Context remind us of this big idea: History repeats itself, generally. So, if we want to create positive change—or if we, at least, want to avoid repeating mistakes—we must do so intentionally by being conscious of the past. They remind us that everything we do causes a ripple in time and that every moment matters.

Why Should We Care

In times of chaos, discord, and dysfunction, and when things go off-course, people with Context provide stability and calm. Their minds naturally return to the preliminary plan, the original vision, and focus on the initial intent. This can be liberating and inspiring because, in times of confusion, they remind us why we started in the first place. It is natural for them to see the underlying structure of the world and to remember how things were. When verbalized, this looks a lot like teaching and can help others see and make sense of the world. Their strength is one of history rather than theory. This means that they generally know, with certainty, what has and has not worked; and if they don't know, they are willing to do the work to find out. In this way, they are people who build firm foundations. More often than not, they have reputations for being reliable, straight-forward, and competent. They also have good memories—for them, there is rarely a need to reinvent the wheel or to try a new approach "just because"—if something worked the last time, they are prone to stick with it. Overall, people with Context are particularly good at keeping situations level and grounded. They shed light on present progress by illuminating the ground we've already covered. They unite us by bringing us back to our core, our roots.

Ten Things to Know About People with CONTEXT

1.   History. They love the past. Instead of feeling help captive, they feel liberated by it. For them, history is a giant gift—it makes everything easier—because it makes the world a more manageable size. We need not try and fail ourselves if someone else has already proven that there is a better way.

2.   Preambles. Folks with Context often give the backstory before saying what they want to say. It is important for them to feel like others know where they are coming from and why.

3.   Strategy. They are people with clear intentions who prefer to know the plan in advance. Even if it changes along the way, they really like to know what the original blueprint, design, or gameplan was.

4.   Cherry Picking. While they can seem overly cautious at times, their perspectives are largely positive. They want to make the present more fully alive and relevant by evoking the past. In a way, their plans are built around only the best of the past and their actions are founded in a knowledge of and appreciation for what works.

5.   Accepting. People with Context have a knack for understanding where people are

coming from. They can quickly connect the dots to determine why a person might be acting or interacting in a certain way. For this reason, they can remain authentically objective, even during intense exchanges, and they don't generally take things personally.

6.   Patterns. They are incredibly good at identifying patterns accurately. It isn't likely that they will spend time trying to find what isn't there.

7.   Proof. They are particularly fond of empirical evidence and concrete proof. It is easier for them to form the basis of their worldview around things that are solid, tangible, and repeatable. The "scientific method" is of particular relevance to them.

8.   Unease. Being self-aware, they will make every effort to lead with intention and to act with purpose. For them, it is important to always know what they are doing and why they are doing it. Without that clarity they can feel very uncomfortable, even anxious. Lack of direction can easily fill them with existential dread.

9.   Change. Even though they admire the past, they are not stuck in it. In fact, they can be enthusiastic early adopters of innovation because their radars are sharp and can identify upcoming

trends and anticipate needs based on similar cycles of change in the past.

10.   Love. Because they naturally look back, they feel strongly connected to others with whom they can reminisce. Conversations in which they relive joyful, passionate, or exciting moments can feel deeply nourishing to them. They enjoy the process of creating meaningful memories.

What Is the FUTURISTIC Theme

Futuristic people are the ones in our lives who naturally dwell in what is possible—their focus is on what could be, not on what is or what has been. In their eyes, the horizon is the most important feature of any landscape, both inner and outer. For them, the future is a source of life as well as a positively grounding force. That is, they make sense of the present—the current moment—based upon a vision of what is to come. Because their perspective centers around possibilities, there is an inextinguishable optimism in their thinking. A situation that feels bleak to others may feel rich with opportunity to Futuristic folks. The future is limitless, undifferentiated potential; it is the spring from which the present moment is constantly flowing. The very idea of it is energizing. So, one of their favorite questions is, "What if?" And, they don't like to stop there, instead they like to figure out how to turn a vision into a reality. It is nourishing for them to bring an idea into such clarity that others, too, can see and experience it. They can be tireless in their innovation, knowing that the world will never be "complete" but it can always be added to and explored further. Through them, we have access to our own and the world's untapped powers. They meet us where we are and then push us to identify what and where we all could be.

Why Should We Care

These are the people who can see that which is on the horizon with vivid clarity. Their instinct is to direct their gaze down the line to see and anticipate what is next; they are very good at predicting things. So, when it comes to being both excited and prepared about what is to come, these people show us the way. They have a particular knack for seeing around corners—and they generally do so with optimism. For them, it is a future of solutions, not problems. They are great with build-from- scratch scenarios and are naturally entrepreneurial. Their vision of the future is unique because it does not dismiss the here and now, instead it places it at one end of a spectrum. That is, the present is a reference point and there can be no future without it—so, their questioning might look like this, "What can we do now to get to what is next?" They teach us how to build bridges through time.

Ten Things to Know About People with FUTURISTIC

1.   Action. While Futuristic is a visionary strength, it is also one of action. It is not enough

for them to just have the big idea, they also need to feel like they are moving toward it, creating it.

2.   Staying Inspired. They may choose to share their big ideas with others, ultimately, because they want to move their vision into reality; and they know that by putting it out there they are creating outside accountability. This staves off procrastination and builds motivation.

3.   The Past. The past is not super interesting to them and it is not likely to be a valuable, or valid, reference point in their thinking. Saying "Remember last time?" or "In the past this didn't work" is not generally significant to them, it may even be annoying.

4.   Persuasion. Because they can see what others cannot, Futuristic people are always developing their art of persuasion—of getting others to see what they see. Sometimes they will go it alone on certain projects, just so that others have something concrete to look at and understand the initial vision.

5.   Presence. Futuristic does not mean 'head in the clouds'. If anything, these people have a greater, more highly tuned impression of the present moment than the average person. This is because they are naturally and continually taking

the elements of the here and now into their calculations about what is to come.

6.   Fear. Left unchecked, their thinking can go both ways. These folks may find themselves with an elaborate and instantaneous ability to envision worst-case scenarios, too. These thoughts can feel intrusive.

7.   Collaboration. They naturally value others' skills because they know that more can always be done together. Finding others who can help take their ideas out of the ether and into the world is always on their radar. For them, witnessing an idea materialize borders on euphoria.

8.   Dismissed. As kids, many people with futuristic were dismissed for their inability to articulate and express the nature of their thoughts, ideas, and impressions. As adults, they may be shy to open up initially, or hold back until they feel that trust has been established.

9.   Claustrophobia. Futuristic people value spaciousness. This means, one, not having their ideas shot down right away and, two, having time and space to play with ideas and envision them from all angles. For them, not be constrained to "what is" is freedom.

10.   Love. Because they love to dwell in possibility, the simple act of dreaming out loud with them can create a powerful sense of closeness. Even asking them to "Say more" can feel like an "I love you."

What Is the IDEATION Theme

Simply put, these are the people in our lives with a passion for ideas. They love to have far-out thoughts and to play with concepts large and small. Testing the limits of an idea, finding its branches, and envisioning all the ways that it could be linked to other parts of the world is the work of ideators. They naturally run with thoughts, often just to see where they go. Intuitively exploring the connections between things, they have a genuine and productive curiosity. For them, an idea is a doorway—not an endpoint—it is an entrance to more. Ideas lead to ideas. In that way, their world is limitless, interconnected, and highly synaptic. More than anything, they love to be fascinated and to wonder at things, to be awestruck and mesmerized. In this way, their thinking is prismatic: imagine clear light entering into their brains and rainbow light coming out in all directions. For ideators, the 'point' is not necessarily to always do something with their thinking—in many cases, simply having an idea is enough for them. A good idea anchors them to their own inner richness, their sense of self, and their sense of contribution to the world.

Why Should We Care

People with ideation are profoundly creative thinkers, incessant innovators, and productive brainstormers. When it comes to filling a pipeline with new ideas, connections, and content, we find them enthusiastically engaged and at the ready. They show us other worlds within our own and they take us out of the status quo. For ideators, reality, like the cosmos, is infinite, intricately interconnected, and ever-expanding. They love to see what other ideas are present below the surface and they draw people and organizations out of static thinking. Their enthusiasm can be contagious—an invitation to see the world through their kaleidoscopic eyes. By modeling how expansive one's mind can be, they remind us each of our unique potential.

Ten Things to Know About People with IDEATION

1.   Starting Things. Ideators are great at starting things—it is the part of the process that they find most energizing—and it is their gift. However, as a culture, we are not taught how to value this, and many ideators beat themselves up about "never finishing things."

2.   Vetting. They don't necessarily vet their ideas. Scrutiny can feel limiting, even claustrophobic for them. For, they know that a

seemingly absurd idea can hold the seed of a brilliant one.

3.   Action. All of their ideas are not "to-dos" or "action items". Sometimes it's just thought exploration.

4.   Connecting The Dots. In general, they are objectively smart people and their brains work incredibly fast. They are constantly refining their skill of connecting the dots for others in ways that make sense.

5.   Ambiverts. Many ideators are one part introvert, one part extrovert—a combo which accommodates both their enthusiasm and their depth. They may need to recharge in solitude after a social outing; or, the opposite, they may need stimulation and interaction after a period of isolation.

6.   Feelings. Ideators might try to think their feelings instead of feeling them.

7.   Sensitivity. Ideas are a source of life for ideators, so shooting them down can feel belittling and utterly toxic to them. They have zero respect for closed-mindedness.

8.   Ideating. Sometimes, they may need to engage in really intense and deep conversations. It can be a type of nourishment for them.

9.   Eccentric. Ideators are at home in deep cerebral waters and spend a lot of time in their imaginations. They are inclined to bring up unconventional topics in casual conversations.

10.   Boredom. They are prone to boredom and may even feel it viscerally as a sensation in their body.

What Is the INPUT Theme

These people are the magpies of the Strengths world. They are collectors and curators and have many interests. Folks with input have a generalized curiosity about virtually everything and they seem to enjoy the sort of thinking that allows them to be fascinated, even overwhelmed at times. They love the vastness and intricacy of life, reality, and the world. In that way, they are "Renaissance People" who naturally and reflexively gather objects into collections and mentally register information, memories, and ideas. Not only do they want to see, feel, and experience it all, they also want to remember, share, and keep it all too. What is possibly most important for them is finding a system, a way to archive, catalogue, index, or display what they have gathered. There is an omnipresent sense of 'just-in-case' with them—they can envision a possible use or a possible reason for holding on to basically anything.

These are the people who have ornate filing systems, epic Pinterest pages, beautiful arrays of trinkets on bookshelves, and a virtual tickertape of conversation topics, interesting facts, jokes, stories, and, ideally, exciting memories of their own experiences. They have the capacity to be deeply present listeners, too, picking up on the smallest details of what they hear, intuit, and observe. More than anything else, their sense of scale is highly evolved—they may marvel at the vastness of space one moment and then the complexity of ants working together the next. For them, it is all important; it is all worth their attention and, in most cases, their admiration as well. And so, if it is worth that much, it is also worth saving and/or remembering. They are collectors of things, finders of things, and keepers of things: micro and macro, real or intangible, near and far. They keep us conscious of the infinite.

<u>Why Should We Care</u>

Those with the strength of input are innovative, openly complex, and resourceful people. They have vast stores of information, references, and resources that they are hungry to share. When it comes to working with them, they are walking/talking encyclopedias who help us push projects and visions into a larger context with bigger, broader, and more meaningful connections. Their impulse is to want to relate one thing to another and to find a purpose, a use, or a home for all that they have gathered. They are constantly being "reminded" of things, which is their gift. For, they often reveal important links that turns chaos into order. They have a skill that helps us see the interrelated nature of all things. People with input also help us value the full spectrum, from the beauty of a grain of sand to the very spinning cosmos. They teach us how to be curious about the world. They may even show us how to be in awe.

Ten Things to Know About People with INPUT

1.   Juxtaposition. Folks with input are likely to make leaping connections between things. While it may feel random or disjointed to others, for them there is a logic to it. Don't be afraid to ask them to connect the dots a little bit.

2.   Completism. People with input are completists—they find a value in having all of something or experiencing the entire range of things. If they like a certain musician, for example, it's likely that they will try to own or listen to everything that the artist has produced.

3.   Good Tastes. Because of their completist nature, they are great refiners of things and have good tastes—especially in the arts, music, film, literature, restaurants, and entertainment. Because they've seen it all, we can reliably look to them for great recommendations.

4.   Analogies. They are very associative people, prone to making sense of the world by exploring one thing's relationship to another. They may use a lot of analogies.

5.   Finishing. They may have a hard time finishing things because they get off track very easily. They may also have a difficult time ever feeling truly finished because of how they dwell in possibility, abundance, variety, and potential.

6.   Netflix. People with input might take binging on shows to an awesome level. The internet serves as a mixed blessing when it comes to their desire for "all-ness".

7.   Input Gone Wild. They can imagine a use or a future use for virtually anything, which can turn into a compulsion to save and store everything that they come into contact with. Input gone wild is hording.

8.   Heavy Topics. It may seem like they want to talk about everything all at once. Don't be surprised if they somehow take a conversation from the light and airy to the deep and philosophical.

9.   Novelty. They have a deep reverence for what is new to them. They rarely re-read or re-watch things, they may even hesitate to go to the same places twice because, for them, the world is so large and there is so much else that they haven't seen.

10.   Useless Information. They may refer to themselves at "troves of useless information". This playful self-deprecation can come from a lifetime of being dismissed. People with input feel valued when they are given the opportunity to have stream-of-consciousness conversations.

What Is the INTELLECTION Theme

People with the Strength of Intellection are the truly deep thinkers in our lives who love to muse, reflect, and explore the landscapes of the mind. They are able to think and process in multiple dimensions simultaneously and seem to love the effort of applying mental energy to life—at times, to the point of befuddlement or exhaustion. In a phrase: They love to think and dive deep. And, small talk is really not their thing. Regardless of the situation or time of day, whether actively or passively, they are always contemplating, brainstorming, or mulling over something. There is a mental hunger present at all times. They are generally reflective and intelligent people who like to be fascinated, to wonder, and to be quietly awed. They may attempt to "think" their feelings, which, at times, makes them feel inaccessible. While typically prone to introversion, they can be very passionate and engaging when it comes to their ideas. While they can be characterized as cerebral, pensive, and heady, their primary motivation is actually curiosity, which fuels their endless hunt for mental activity. For them, the world seems to be an extension of their brain—a type of holding place for more thoughts. In that way, they draw out the best of our own thinking by encouraging us to go deeper into our own mental world. Their presence cheers a greater awareness, allowing the light of mind to reflect through. People with Intellection can make the abstract tangible and give us greater access to the invisible world all around us.

Why Should We Care

When it comes to taking an idea to the next level by exploring it from every angle, those with Intellection are among the best. It is their instinct to go deep with thoughts—the surface is boring to them. Experts in mentally peeling back the layers of a given challenge or concept, they reveal options, choices, and opportunities that may have been previously unseen or unseeable. Folks with Intellection are good foundation builders and are particularly skilled at scaling up ideas and filling pipelines. They curate a depth of understanding— be it macro or micro, focused or broad. In many cases, they effortlessly nourish an appreciation for the worlds complexities—as opposed to a disdain for them. This shift in focus allows for clarity and then concrete actions to occur. They ask us to look into challenges as opposed to look away from them. They open our field of awareness, help us create solutions, and remind us that wonder can be generative.

Ten Things to Know About People with INTELLECTION

1.   Productivity. For them, being productive does not necessarily mean "doing" something. Sitting down to think, reflect, and process is likely to be viewed as a highly valuable use of their time. Then, once they've mapped something out in their mind, they can generally make quick work of it.

2.   Philosophical. Discussing philosophies, theories, systems, concepts, and literature can be extremely fulfilling to people with Intellection. Questions that cannot be answered have a particular appeal and they like to entertain many angles of a thought without accepting or rejecting a specific one.

3.   On/On. It seems that they are always— ALWAYS—thinking. Even if it is, at times, happening quietly in the background of their minds—there is always an inner-awareness of the mental activity lighting up their brains, which are perpetually growing.

4.   Boredom. Being mentally stimulated is a key source of life for them. From crossword puzzles to intense conversations about the meaning of life, they create ways to stay connected, focused, and inspired. Boredom is not

an option, and they may feel it more intensely than others.

5.   Introversion. As introspection is at the core of this theme, folks with Intellection often prefer some time alone each day. They are generally comfortable spending extended periods of quality time in solitude.

6.   Mental Empathy. The way that an empath tunes in and feels the emotions of others, people with Intellection channel the mental activity of others. They are excellent trackers of ideas and flows of ideas. They can deeply understand the ways that others think, process, and respond to life.

7.   Digesting. At times, they might share an idea that seems either "far out" or non-sequitur. Generally, this is because they've already spent time working it out in their mind and have seen it mentally from all angles. Don't be surprised if they hold the rest of us to a high standard, asking us to truly understand and appreciate their ideas.

8.   Learning. For them, it isn't so much about learning things as it is about challenging their mind and exploring things. Existential ideation, deep thoughts, new ideas, brain games, imagining, and wondering out loud can serve as solid nourishment for them.

9.   Depth. They seem to be able to find a greater depth to almost anything. This stimulates and feeds their sense of wonder and astonishment. They generally dislike being asked to scale it back. Being told that "everything doesn't have to be so complicated" or "deep" will likely annoy them.

10.   Love. Thinking big, making big plans, thinking outside the box, and having deep conversations will go a long way in creating a genuine connection with them. Their love and expressions of it will, too, have a depth and multidimensional qualities.

What Is the LEARNER Theme

Learners love to learn. Yes. But, there is more to it than that. They seem to be following an invisible thread. Learners are the people in our lives who are always digging into something new, researching an idea or topic, and gathering information from anywhere they can. They find tremendous value and pleasure in traveling from ignorance to deeper levels of awareness. Experiencing the world as it opens around a new subject is a near-sacred pursuit for them. However, not just any old subject; for learners, there needs to be a spark of natural interest. They are not people who are "happy to learn anything". No, they must be drawn in, and the newer the knowledge is, the better. Even if it seems like their interests pull them in ten directions, their thirst is intuitively guided and they are very much at home in it.

Why Should We Care

Learners are actively engaged in life and they teach us how see the world with hunger and interest. They see layers and depth where the rest of the world may see only the surface. Learners remind us that life is a precious opportunity to grow and to do something substantial. They are the ones who dive in, as they are not easily threatened by newness. In the workplace and in our communities, they are positive disruptors and changemakers. They naturally shake things up, asking us to dig deeper, rise up, and ask questions.

Ten Things to Know About People with LEARNER

1. Rabbit Holes. The internet might very well be the universe's personal gift to learners, who are prone to 'following their nose' down rabbit holes of ideas. This experience can be euphoric for them.

2. Studenting. If learners could be full-time college students forever, they would. So, don't be surprised if they treat life itself like a type of classroom—taking notes, seeking feedback, asking lots of questions, studying, digging deeper, and even citing sources in casual conversation.

3. Hummingbirds. Learners can be a lot like hummingbirds deeply investigating one subject and then quickly moving on to the next one. While this may seem random, there is usually a meaningful connection or reason for the learner as they move from one realm into another.

4. Preparedness. Regardless of how much they've researched and prepped, learners might never feel properly prepared for an event, speech, or presentation. Don't be surprised if it seems like they are always preparing, preparing, preparing.

5.   Excellence. Learners are magnetically drawn to experts. They love to spend time around them, absorbing and asking questions.

6.   Dissatisfied. Because their passion and thirst for deeper and deeper levels of competency and understanding can override their ability appreciate how much they actually do know, learners have a tendency to focus on how much they don't know.

7.   Rewards. Often, the process of learning is more akin to exploring and the act itself is a reward for them. They are likely to be irritated by the question, "So, what are you going to do with that knowledge?"

8.   Motto. When it comes to knowledge, a learner's motto might be "If a little is good, a lot

must be better." Again, they are reaching for an ever-expanding level of awareness.

9.   Others. Learners can be viewed as intense, almost reckless in their pursuit of a topic. What they desire is someone to connect with at a shared level of intensity. When this need is not being met by anyone in their network learners can feel unseen, misunderstood, and undervalued.

10.   The Holy Moment. Learners may hold to the idea that someday, somehow it will ALL come together and everything they have ever learned will jell into a coherent, intricately interconnected whole.

What Is the STRATEGIC Theme

These are the people in our lives who have the gift of instantaneously seeing the world as it could be. Strategic people are naturally adept at identifying options, weighing them, and confidently making a decision. They are action-oriented and solution-focused. They do not dwell in life's 'problems'—in fact, they generally see opportunities where others see only chaos and crisis. They are incredibly fast processors who rely on their ability to notice and remember patterns in people, places, and things.

Strategic people can mentally move through a situation playing out multiple scenarios and outcomes simultaneously; this helps them make sense of what is at stake. From there, they make decisions with ease and confidence because they've already played the tapes, seen the possibilities, and understand the various moving parts. They see in multiple dimensions simultaneously.

Why Should We Care

Strategic people are wayseers. Where others find roadblocks, they find inroads to innovation, progress, and resolution. At a crossroads, they help us see the potential in ourselves, others, and in the world.

They are extremely resourceful, often creating elegant solutions to complex problems. They strategize seemingly effortlessly; the process of assessing situations, envisioning outcomes, and taking action is definitely in their comfort zone— it may even be soothing for them. They help us and our teams make critical decisions and move forward because they are not afraid—they assess, decide, and take action.

Ten Things to Know About People with STRATEGIC

1.   Thinking In Chunks. Strategic people process information rapidly and in batches— think waves instead of droplets. In fact, at times they seem to simply download information fully-formed from the ether.

2.   Perspective. While the word 'strategic' might imply something cerebral, it is actually a particular

perspective that these people embody—a specific way of seeing the world, not just thinking about it.

3.   Problems. For strategic people, there are not really any problems, only solutions.

4.   Knowing. Strategic people operate from a deep place of just knowing and they generally feel

bothered by having to explain the hows and whys of their thinking. Asking "How do you know?" is annoying to them because they generally cannot show their work (i.e. A + B = C).

5.   Best Path. They are not married to one way of doing things—if they conceive of a better path forward, they are happy to shift gears, turn the wheel, and take it.

6.   Giving Up. They do not give up easily. Because they can see so many possibilities and options they generally push through, even after others have lost faith.

7.   Streamlining. They always have an eye out for how a process can be made better or more efficient. They may even have a fondness for tinkering with things.

8.   Creativity. Their thinking has an element of creativity that is easily overlooked. This is because their ideas may seem very straightforward, even obvious, despite the fact that they were the only person to think of it.

9.   Peripheral Vision and Peripheral Hearing. Don't be surprised if a strategic person is deeply aware of absolutely everything that is happening in a room. They generally have great peripheral

vision and hearing, like little radars always scanning spaces quietly.

10.   Trust. Strategic people love to be trusted. Most of them have spent an exhausting amount of energy trying to explain their 'knowing'. For them, being trusted in their decisions is like being truly seen.

SECTION TWO: BUILDING A STRENGTHS MINDSET

Strengths and Differences

Lots of things are easy to know logically but difficult to understand emotionally.

Take, for example, the fact that everyone is different.

It doesn't take a PhD to understand that idea and to know that it's true. Basically, no one is the same.

But, to accept it? To really, truly accept this fact and live in continued awareness of it? That is another question.

That is, can we really learn to accept others for who they are? What are the exceptions, if not? It might sound crazy, but doesn't this idea speak to the core of virtually all human-to-human challenges?

That is, the fact that others view the world differently can be a big problem for us at times.

This idea can be seen clearly in political and social contexts just by turning on the news. There generally isn't just one right answer because there isn't just one worldview.

The idea can be scaled back to its frustratingly simple explanation: Everyone is different.

True, that statement *all by itself* doesn't get us very far.

However, when this idea is intermingled with all of our thoughts in every situation, we develop an awareness *and* an acceptance of others, which is invaluable. From there, we are less likely to be startled by differences and frustrated or turned-off by them.

Instead, we can say, "I already knew that. So, where shall we go from here?" and we can more easily create inroads to collaboration, compromises, and solutions.

Life probably isn't about only being surrounded by people whom we agree with and who agree with us. If that were the case, innovation would be impractical. We would all agree and nothing would shift.

Instead, we seem encouraged at every turn to challenge our beliefs, test our mettle, adapt to changing landscapes, and thrive in virtual and literal unknowns.

Our strengths are our deepest qualities, which serve as inner beacons in this process. They are the fundamental elements of our core—they are concrete identifiers of who we are and how we view life. These qualities make us different and similar to others, in turns.

When we strive to see people as operating from this core, not out of spite or difficulty, but because it is *who they are*, it becomes easier to accept them as that: themselves.

Each strength is like a gear in a watch. Any good timepiece has multiple sprockets of various shapes and sizes, and *no extra parts.* Everything is there for a specific reason. One gear is not better than the other or more important, because each one contributes to the functioning of the whole.

That is the same with us and our strengths. We each have different shaped sprockets to add to the grand scheme. When we begin looking for how the differences in others can *help* us, as opposed to *threaten* us, then we are open to options and solutions that were previously unavailable.

Three Questions

What are the five most important qualities in a person?

What are five words that I hope people associate with me?—Kind, generous, loving, funny, etc.

What is the best memory from my life?

Action

Write a letter that you will never send. Pick one person in your life and write them a greatness letter. This is a letter that praises them to the fullest—let it be over-the-top and gushing. Tell them every wonderful thing that you have ever wanted to tell them. Let it all out.

Take the letter when you are done and seal it in an envelope. You may chose to throw it away or recycle it or burn it. The point is to write a letter that has no restrictions, one where you are uninhibited and can say everything that your have ever wanted to say without worrying about how the person will receive it.

How to Start a Writing Practice that Produces Lasting Positive Change

The point of starting a writing practice is to explore your mind, your thinking, and your life in a new way.

Writing is one way to develop the brain and test its limits—the same way that athletes do cardio, train with weights, and eat with intention—variety is important. This is to say that writing is just one piece in an overall healthy brain. Other components include thinking, problem solving, working, playing, dreaming, imagining, exercise and nutrition.

In some ways, freewriting is the easiest way to challenge the brain because there is no right or wrong way to do it. All that is important is that it is done. So, allow your writing practice to surprise you. Don't put any artificial limits or expectations on it. That said, here are a few tips:

Start small and remove expectations.
Start small. Begin with 4-5 mins per day. This helps to develop the habit. It's only 5 mins per day...that's .00347% of one day! Starting small also creates an understanding that writing doesn't "have" to be anything. Your writing practice should be a stress free and relaxed process.

Be consistent and commit to it.
Commit to 5 minuets a day for 30 days. If you are not impressed after a month, you can stop. No one is forcing any of this.

Use prompts.
Prompts give the mind a starting place, like a springboard into bigger ideas. Don't restrict yourself to staying on the prompt, allow your thinking and your pen to wander. Oftentimes, your mind will stumble upon great truths.

Look below the surface for clues.
Our brains have comfort zones. These are ideas that they prefer to consider and return to time and time again. Good, bad, or ugly, our brains have a hard time letting go of some beliefs, even if they are unproductive to our overall vision of life. As you progress in your writing practice, it won't take long to skim your entries and find patterns and habits in your thoughts. (This is also why it's good to be consistent). Reviewing your work is a great way to identify possible obstacles present in your thinking that are holding you back from growing, changing, and evolving. Remember, it's difficult to change what you don't know is there. Freewriting brings a lot of ideas to the surface for examination—it can be surprising!

Questions Worth Asking: 50 Days Worth of Prompts:

- What would my perfect day look like?
- What is my best quality?
- In what ways am I similar to how I was as a kid?
- What are the details of my dream house?
- Would I want to win the lottery? Why or why not?
- How is the world different today than it was 100 years ago?
- Why do we watch TV?
- What are five things that I like about myself?
- What are three ways that I add value to the lives of those around me?
- In what ways do I add value to the world at large?
- If I were offered a trip to explore Mars, would I go? What if it were only one way?
- Am I holding on to any grudges?
- What are the most important qualities in a friend?
- Who are my mentors, who do I look up to and why?
- What is the tone of my inner monologue?
- What is my general outlook on life?
- What are my core beliefs about why I am here?

- What types of messages do I repeat to myself throughout the day?
- What is the purpose of my life?
- What action can I take today to feel better about my life?
- What obstacles do I see in my way?
- What is my biggest fear?
- How do I cope with stress?
- What are five things that I would like to see more of in my life?
- What are some qualities in others that I admire?
- What is my adult version of playtime?
- Do I like to be alone? Why or why not?
- What does it mean to feel balanced?
- How old do I think I will live to be?
- What do I do with my freetime?
- How often do I use the phrase, "I should..."
- What are my favorite subjects to talk about with others?
- What types of things do I want to learn more about?
- What types of conversations make me cringe?
- What do I actively avoid talking about with others?
- What are five ways that I could practice better self-love and self-care?

- What action could I take before the day is over to practice one of the above?
- Who are my five heroes in life (people who I know personally)?
- Who are my five heroes in life (famous, historical, or otherwise)?
- What qualities do my heroes embody that I, too, would like to develop?
- If I were an animal, which one would I be and why?
- How is the modern world changing and what do I think about it?
- If I were on a desert island, what five objects would I bring and why?
- Will computers ever be smarter and more capable than humans?
- If aliens landed and asked me to show them around, where would I start?
- What is the most important (non-essential) activity in a person's life?
- Have I been living from my strengths?
- Where do I see myself in 5 years? 10 years? 20 years?
- What is the meaning of life?
- If I were to get in a rocket ship and travel straight up, how far could I go? How far is up?

Strengths and Returning to Basics

When we focus on what is going right instead of what is going wrong, our perspective changes and we are able to live fuller, more productive and satisfying lives.

This does not mean turning a blind eye to life's challenges. No. Instead, it is a call to develop a greater awareness of one thing: *our focus*.

That means, when we pattern our thinking around strengths, we liberate ourselves from limiting, self-defeating beliefs and perspectives. Developing a strengths focus and mentality helps us sort through and prioritize which thoughts and actions contribute to our best self and which keep us static and locked in fear or indecision.

Difficult as it may be to consider, some of our ideas about the world are probably outdated and could use some revision. The strengths give us productive tools to reevaluate our lives and our thinking with. That's because they provide a comprehensive language to use, one which describes concrete actions to take toward change.

It's worth stating that, perhaps, at one point in our life certain views and beliefs were relevant, but not any longer. Our feelings of fear, lack, or insecurity, for example, are likely grounded in real and practical experiences, which are long over but still echoing in our lives today.

By focusing on our strengths, we are freeing ourselves to move forward from a place of competence, confidence, and positive momentum.

Living from our strengths develops an awareness that we don't *have* to be anyone else because...we already *are* someone. The strengths teach us how to honor and love who we already are, first and foremost; and then, with that knowledge, we learn how to become more and more of that.

The model of "focusing on weaknesses" teaches us how to become *less and less* bad at things.

The model of "focusing on strengths" teaches us how to become more and more and better and better at things that we are already good at and strong in. That, in itself, is greatness.

Three Questions

What does my happiness look like?

Am I happy?

What is one action that I could take today toward a greater and more complete happiness?

Action

Break out your phone and send three "just because" text messages to three people in your life. The messages can be short and sweet. A simple, "Hi. I was just thinking of you. I hope you are doing well!" will do.

Try it. See what happens.

NEVER STOP
FIGHTING UNTIL
YOU ARRIVE AT
YOUR DESTINED
PLACE--THAT IS THE
UNIQUE YOU.

A.P.J. ABDUL KALAM

Strengths and Outcomes

We've all heard the saying: A journey of a thousand miles begins with a single step. And, it's true, to reach a destination—any destination—we must first leave where we are.

To take this idea a step further, consider this: We could safely drive from New York to LA in the dark only seeing the 300 or 400 feet in front of us lit by the headlights.

In both cases it boils down to one word: START. That is, we don't need to see the *end* in order to *begin*. But we *do* need to begin in order to finish.

Right?

We can't know all the details of our various journeys in life, so it's important that this doesn't prevent us from setting out. After all, it's easy to get bogged down in all the "hows" of an idea and to forget that life generally unfolds when we allow it.

However, when we try to control every outcome and foresee every obstacle, we generally spend a lot of energy fretting over how we might resolve imaginary challenges.

Instead we can put that energy into preparing the way and creating opportunities in the present.

Our strengths have a lot to say about this idea, too. By identifying our gifts and focusing on them, we know that we can start from *strength* and grow *stronger*, as opposed to starting from "weakness" and hoping to end at strength. Which is a gamble.

When our perspectives are strengths based, we don't need to focus on what is ten miles down the road because the value of what is right in front of us is seen clearly.

The strengths keep us present and prevent us from the discouraging thought of "how, how, how" because we are focused on the encouraging thought of "now, now, now".

3 Questions

What is my next first step?

Do I focus on LA when I haven't even left New York?

What is my ultimate dream for the coming year?

5 Minute Action

Make a list of ten goals you have for the coming year—anything from health and wellness goals to financial goals and relationships.

Find a glass jar and four rolls of pennies.

Dump three rolls into the jar and then add another 65 pennies from the fourth roll.

That gives you 365 pennies in the jar.

Tape your list of ten goals to the outside of the jar and take one penny out every day—starting on January 1st.

Allow the visual representation of time passing in shrinking penny-jar to motivate you.

As your penny count gets lower and lower your list should get shorter and shorter as you accomplish each goal.

Strengths and Awareness and Discovery

The strengths are not about self-help, they are about self-awareness.

By developing a strengths mindset—one where we focus on what we do best and become better at it—we put ourselves on the path of self-discovery. In doing so, we see how present our strengths really are in our lives on both conscious and unconscious levels.

On a conscious level, we can observe our strengths manifesting in our actions. A person with a lot of woo, for example, can be seen mingling and charming those around them; likewise, we take note of the developers in our lives as they help us strategize toward success or resolve.

That said, on an *unconscious* level, we can observe that our emotional state and wellbeing can be in direct relationship to how much *and* how often we find ourselves in the strengths zone.

Experiencing frustration, feelings of lack, and anxiety can all be unconscious reactions to lives in which we are constantly repressing our best selves—be it at work, in relationships, or elsewhere.

So, living in our strengths is *not* about learning something new and then practicing it. No.

Instead, living a strengths life is about developing an awareness of what is already there, and acting in it with a greater intention and consciousness.

Plato believed that we were each born knowing everything there is to know...only, we don't realize it. This idea is called Platonic epistemology.

In this theory, all learning becomes a form of recollection and all of life becomes a long form of remembering.

Our teachers along the way just help us recognize what we already know. The better the teacher, the more they put us in touch with what was always inside of us.

For this reason, our life's greatest teachers are not always found in the classroom.

Add to all this that the root of our word *education* comes from the Latin word *educare*, which means "to lead out of", and it's beginning to look like personal growth is more about developing awareness than it is about anything external.

Three Questions

What is the single most important discovery I have made in my life?

What are three skills I would like to develop in the next 365 days?

What is standing between me and my dream life?

5 Minute Action

Make a list of all the things that you do *not* know. Let your mind wander and play for five minutes.

Remember there is no "right" or "wrong" way to do these exercises. Allow your strengths to guide you in your questioning and your list-making— someone who is very analytical is likely to navigate toward different unknowns than someone who is active in ideation. It's all good!

Sometimes examining what isn't is just as revealing as examining what is. That is, by looking at what we *do not* know, we are likely to discover something new, important, and possibly essential.

Strengths and What's Underneath

A French scientist by the name of Pascal Cotte recently developed a technology that he believes has revealed the true identity of the Mona Lisa once and for all.

Interestingly, it isn't by looking *at* the painting that he forms his conclusions, instead it's by looking *inside* of it.

His device uses a multispectral camera to detect and analyze each layer of paint on a canvas, some of which are thinner than 1/1000th of an inch.

It works like this: blinding light is projected onto the surface and then its reflections are measured—this is called L.A.M. or Layer Amplification Method.

When applied to DaVinci's masterpiece, this process revealed *three other* separate and complete portraits *under* the final version of the Mona Lisa.

Some believe them to be sketches that the artist used to think-out his final composition. Others think that it's all hype and some sort of hoax.

Either way, the idea of an *inner*-Layer Amplification Method seems appealing...as, living from our strengths might do just that.

This is to say that spending time thinking about our best self has the potential to reveal layers of our personality that lie under the surface.

And, the more we think about a thing, the more likely we are to find it.

That is, if we consider each strength as a "layer," then the more time we spend focusing on it, the more its qualities are amplified, brought to the surface, and made visible.

Importantly, it's likely that we've all been told at some point that one of our strengths is a "weakness". Perhaps, if we were told this often enough, we began to believe it. And, in doing so, we added a false layer to cover it up.

Overtime, we create lots and lots of layers—some productive, others not—and our daily devotion to a strengths life is an invitation to dig down and re-discover qualities and gifts that may have been quieted, even silenced, long ago.

When we do this, we can often feel valuable parts of ourselves waking up.

We may not even recognize them any more, but the strengths give us a language to name them and, in some cases, re-name them for what they are: our greatness!

Three Questions

Why is the Mona Lisa so famous in the first place?

Does it matter that there is a painting *underneath* the final product?

What are some of my many layers—how would I describe them?

5 Minute Action

Have you ever tried drawing your own portrait...with your eyes closed?

It's easy and (usually) pretty funny—it's also surprisingly good for relieving stress.

Grab a pen and a piece of paper. Close your eyes and go.

Really commit to not opening them until you are finished. (Fight the impulse to peek!)

When you are done, take a look at what you've created. There are often interesting characteristics revealed about how we see and perceive ourselves (even with our eyes closed).

For example, do you totally forget to include a body part—an eye, a nose, hair? Or, did you exaggerate one specific part of your face? Did you draw yourself with a smile or a frown or without teeth?

What can our portraits say about how we see and feel about our lives?

Strengths and Solutions

John Lennon perfectly describes a strengths mindset when he says, "There are no problems, only solutions."

And, while this idea may seem perplexing at first, when we look at the core of his thought, he's simply talking about perspective.
Are we focused on the problem or are we focused on the solution?

In the same way that we cannot *simultaneously* see both sides of a single coin, we cannot see problems and solutions simultaneously. We can pay attention to one *or* the other, but not both at once.

Now, consider this line of thinking when it comes to living from our strengths.

Are we focused on what we do best or on what we consider to be our struggles?

This, too, is related to our perspective.

We might then say, with the right perspective, "There are no weaknesses, only strengths."

One of the best actions we can take is to develop a greater awareness of our strengths and how we can embody them more fully in our daily lives.

We can do this by checking in with ourselves at regular intervals and simply asking, "Am I living from my strengths?" When done consistently, this action becomes second-nature and we begin to live fluidly from a state of strength.

The moment we take action—any action—to better our lives and improve our situation, we begin living in the solution.

This is because we cannot be *both* problem-minded *and* solution-minded. Just as, we cannot be both strong *and* weak at the same moment. When we focus on solutions, we no longer have problems...we have only solutions.
When we focus on strengths, we find that we only have strengths.

Three Questions

What are my strengths?

What makes me feel most alive?

What action can I take today to feel more alive—even if it's something as "small" as putting an activity on the calendar, or sending an email, or taking a quick walk.

5 Minute Action

Letter from Your 100 Year Old Self to Your Present Self

It's simple: Imagine yourself at age 100 and consider the advice that you would give yourself about your life right now.

This exercise can help provide perspective on the challenges of today.

After all, can't we all look back on our "problems" from 5, 10, even 20 years ago and say, "If I knew then what I know now..."

Because we are asked to grow from any challenge, when we overcome it and change we are able to look back with wiser eyes—which is a perspective we earn only by making it to the other side of any obstacle.

What are your obstacles today and what type of attitude would your 100 year old self advise you to take?

Strengths and Timing: Why Our Strengths Don't Always Feel Like Strengths

A flashlight is fairly pointless outside in the middle of the day.

A bag filled with $100 bills is pretty worthless alone on a deserted island.

And, a dictionary that translates German to Mongolian is useless to an English speaker in Spain.

But, just because these items are not useful to these specific people in these *specific* situations, it doesn't mean that they are all together worthless. Of course not.

A German to Mongolian dictionary would be plenty useful to someone from Frankfurt in Ulaanbaatar. A flashlight instantly becomes valuable when the sun goes down. And, who wouldn't want a bag filled with $100s to show up in their car on the way to the bank?

Just because we don't have a particular use for a given item in one moment, doesn't mean we write it off for good as trash. If that were the case, we would all throw away our snow blowers, gloves, and sweaters when spring came. And then buy them all again next winter.

While that might be good for businesses, it would be insane to behave in that way.

So, when it comes to *objects* we all have a clear sense that there is an appropriate time and place for each of them. And, depending on the circumstances, its specific and practical value emerges, ebbs, and flows. We don't devalue the flashlight as an object because it doesn't necessarily serve a specific function *all* the time.

Our strengths function according to this principle, too. We might not *always* be able to use *all* of our strengths at full volume in every situation all the time. No way.

But, learning when and where to use our strengths is as important as learning when and where to use a bullhorn or a hammer or a jumprope.

When used in the right places at the right time, our strengths can make us superhuman. And, knowing when and where and how much to engage them is an art. One that we learn through trial and error and by consciously developing a strengths mindset.

While we cannot necessarily turn our strengths *on* or *off*, we can develop an awareness of when, where, and how we can best serve a given situation and then throttle our contributions up or down accordingly.

This exercise allows us to practice the principles of listening to others and observing the world around us, which creates a spirit of teachability and resourcefulness.

When we try to impose our strengths on others as the *only* way, not only are we denying those others *their* strengths, but we are also denying ourselves the gifts of what others' strengths can teach us.

Three Questions

When was a time that I was in the right place at the right time?

What are five words that describe my "zone"?

What is more important when meeting someone new: listening or talking?

5 Minute Action

Take Five Minutes to Eat One Square of Chocolate

Find a bar of your favorite chocolate—dark, milk, with almonds, with chili peppers, etc.

Break one square off.

Set the timer on your phone.

Allow five minute to pass between the time you begin eating it and the final, last bite.

Take notes about your thoughts and your process for this action. What does your approach reveal about you? What other methods can you think of for making a square of chocolate last for five mins?

For example, did you nibble consistently or did you chomp and wait, chomp and wait? Why did you chose the method that you did? Do you operate in a similar manner elsewhere?

Was this fun, stressful, insightful, pointless, weird, enlightening? Why or why not?

SOMETIMES IT'S THE
JOURNEY THAT
TEACHES YOU A LOT
ABOUT YOUR
DESTINATION.

DRAKE

Strengths and Self-Acceptance | Part 1

A core belief in developing a strengths mindset is this: As we grow we will become more of who we already are; we are going to grow and develop most in our areas of strength.

Think of it this way: A flamingo could go its entire life trying to become a penguin and never succeed. A flamingo can only become more of what it is—a better and better flamingo.

When we spend our physical, emotional, mental, and spiritual energies trying to be someone else, not only are we denying what we *truly* are, we are not growing and evolving along the lines that we were meant to grow and evolve upon.

After all, we might spend all of our time and energy trying to get *moderately* good at something that simply comes naturally to someone else—our thousand hours to their ten. If we can learn to accept our selves and our strengths, we can practice developing them and focusing on their evolution.

This is, however, where it gets tricky. Because, in order to become *more* of what we are, we must first *know* what we are! We must first become aware of our foundation—and from there we can grow. As always, by becoming more aware of what lights up and feels good (as opposed to what we are told by others or society) we put ourselves in a position to experience self-discovery. To do this, we must begin asking ourselves questions and begin searching for answers. One of the most powerful questions we can ask ourselves is this: Really, truly, how am I doing and feeling about life?

Three Questions

Do I truly know who I am and what my life's purpose is?

Is there someone in my life that I could brainstorm this question with?

What are three things that I love about myself in this moment?

An Action

Desired Result: Give a Gift To Your Future Self

Concrete Action: Hide Positive Messages, Gifts, and Notes for Your Future Self to Find

Have you ever found $20 in your pocket that you didn't know was there? Or, have you ever stumbled across an old letter or photograph that makes you feel good? I think that we all love it when that happens. This action creates conditions where that can occur more regularly in life. It's pretty easy to imagine how it works. Gather up five or ten mementos, photos, ten dollar bills, letter, notes, and/or nick-knacks, and put them in a pile. Then, have a trusted friend or family member and, while you are not in the room, have them hide these objects around your space. Make them vow to never tell you where they put them. Then, simply go on living. In the back of your mind you will know that there are these little "gifts" hiding out in your space, but you don't know when or where you will find them. If you don't have a friend who will go along with this (and you have a short memory) try hiding them yourself.

Strengths and Self-Acceptance | Part 2

Accepting who we are simply means never having to pretend that we are something that we are not, which can take *a lot* of energy.

By embracing ourselves and all of our humanness we can shift our focus from perfection to *progress*. And, when we look for it, we are always making progress, even if it appears in millimeters.

Accepting ourselves in this moment for all that we are in this moment—as well as all that we have been in the past—does not mean giving up and "accepting" that we will forever stay the same. In fact, it can mean the opposite. It can mean freedom.

Learning to acknowledge and name what we are experiencing assists in identifying the obstacles in our way, which are keeping us "the same". From there, we can almost always envision a new path to move *forward* on.

So, how do we do that? We can start by learning to accept who we have been. And we can do that quietly by naming our feelings when they are brought to the surface. For example, say that a memory makes us feel embarrassed or angry. What we can do is pause and quietly state, "That made me feel embarrassed or angry. Since then, I have felt lots of other emotions. I don't need to reactivate this feeling in this present moment. I don't need to re-feel it now. I can accept that I felt it in the past and I can leave it there."

Three Questions

What is my favorite memory from this life?

When am I truly my happiest self?

If I had to pick between having four arms or four legs, which would I choose and why?

An Action

Desired Result: Be Happier

Concrete Action: Start a Laughing Practice

We've all heard of yoga and meditation practices, so what about a laughing practice? That is, a time set aside each day to laugh. Here's how you do it. Sit at the edge of your bed, set your phone timer for 60 seconds, close your eyes, and begin to fake laugh to the best of your ability. If you really go for it, it will likely turn into real laughter. And then that happens you get all the health benefits of real and true JOY. Note: Because the body cannot recognize fake laughter from real laughter, even if you fake laugh for a full minute, you still:

Strengthen your heart. When we laugh we are taking in huge breaths of air. That oxygen surge relaxes the body, increases blood flow, and improves the function of blood vessels.

Boost your immune system. When we laugh, we decrease stress hormones, like cortisol, which increases the production of immune cells and infection-fighting antibodies.

Release the body's pharmacy of feel-goods. When we laugh, we release endorphins, which make us feel happy and can even block pain.

Strengths and Self-Acceptance | Part 3

Thinking about self-acceptance and experiencing a greater amount of it doesn't need to be a mushy-gushy process. It's mostly a conversation that we have with ourselves about our self-limiting beliefs and how to overcome them.

After all, we cannot address a challenge, obstacle, or *limit* until we acknowledge it, name it, and accept that it's there. So, we overcome our self-limits with self-acceptance. Once we've accepted a thing, we can consciously do something about it.

Just as there is a language for our strengths, there is a language of self-acceptance. It can sound a few ways—mainly, it uses words and ideas framed around the principles of: patience, teachability, humility, and courage.

Taking a look in the mirror and loving ourselves enough to be honest and pro-active requires each of these. Acceptance means being patient as we grow and evolve; being willing to be taught new ways of thinking and acting; having humility enough to see where our lives need work; and having the courage to do something about it.

Putting these ideas into action begins when we ask ourselves in moments of frustration *and* joy,

"Am I being patient, teachable, humble, and courageous?" Like so many lasting changes, they start with a question and evolve into an action. Dive in, fine-tune along the way. Right?

Three Questions

What would my ten-year-old self tell me are my best qualities today?

What would my ninety-year-old self tell me are my best qualities today?

What is my favorite song of all time and why?

An Action

Desired Result: Relieve Boredom

Concrete Action: Play a Private Game of Six Degrees of Separation

Ever notice how one thought connects to the next and then the next and the next until we are somehow thinking about something totally random? It's like, we start thinking about a specific memory or idea and all of a sudden tons of these *other* memories and ideas start coming to the surface. Best part is that you can play a game with this process, and you can do this pretty much anytime and anywhere you find yourself feeling bored. It goes like this: Set the timer on your phone for three minutes, write down a word, any word, and conjure an image of it in your mind and hold it there. Start your timer and then relax your mind, let it run free. Don't try to control where your thinking goes, don't "grab" any thoughts as they float by, just let your mind wander. When your timer goes off, check in with your brain and locate the dominant thought. That is, where did your mind wind up after the three minutes? Write it down next to your original word. Are they the same? Similar? Juxtaposed? Chances are, your mind started in one place and wound up a thousand miles away...in just *three* minutes.

Strengths and Inspiration | Part 1

Food for Thought and Action:

The world around us is created, recreated, shaped, and reshaped by one thing: action. That said, every action in the outer world first began in the inner world.

Awareness leads to thought. Thoughts lead to emotion. Emotions lead to actions. Actions lead to results.

By cutting out the middle-stuff, we can see that our awareness leads directly to our results. So, what we spend our time *thinking* about (aka focusing our awareness upon) has a rippling out, real-world effect.

That's because what we focus on triggers a chain reaction that unavoidably leads to actions—this includes speech, body language, behavior, and anything else that can be observed and sensed by those outside of us.

So, what separates a change maker from the rest of the world? Their awareness. What they focus on. The chain reactions they incite and encourage in their mind. Think about the mindset of the following individuals and ask, "What do they all share in common?"

Khalil Gibran | Esther Abraham Hicks | Marilyn Monroe | Abraham Lincoln | Mother Teresa | John F. Kennedy | Martin Luther King Jr.| Nelson Mandela | William Shakespeare | Winston Churchill | Virginia Woolf | Bill Gates | Muhammad Ali | Mahatma Gandhi | Margaret Thatcher | Charles de Gaulle | Christopher Columbus | George Orwell | Charles Darwin | Elvis Presley | Albert Einstein | Paul McCartney | Plato | Leonardo da Vinci | Robert De Niro | Louis Pasteur | Leo Tolstoy | Pablo Picasso | Vincent Van Gogh | Franklin D. Roosevelt | Thomas Edison | Rosa Parks | Mark Zuckerberg | Ludwig Beethoven | Oprah Winfrey | Indira Gandhi | Eva Peron | Dalai Lama | Walt Disney | Peter Sellers | Barack Obama | Malcolm X | J.K.Rowling | Richard Branson | Pele | Angelina Jolie | Jesse Owens | Harper Lee | Ernest Hemingway | John Lennon | Henry Ford | Michael Jordon | Ingrid Bergman | Oscar Wilde | Coco Chanel | Amelia Earhart | Charlie Chaplin | Sting | Alfred Hitchcock | Michael Jackson | Madonna | Cleopatra | Grace Kelly | Steve Jobs | Babe Ruth | Sigmund Freud | Woodrow Wilson | Katherine Hepburn | Audrey Hepburn | Salvador Dalí | David Beckham | Tiger Woods | Usain Bolt | Carl Lewis | Jacqueline Kennedy Onassis | C.S. Lewis | Billie Holiday |

J.R.R. Tolkien | Anne Frank | Julie Andrew | Florence Nightingale | Marie Curie | Stephen Hawking | Tim Burton | Lance Armstrong | Shakira | Meryl Streep | Jon Stewart | Wright Brothers | Tom Cruise | Rupert Murdoch | Al Gore | Sacha Baron Cohen | George Clooney | Kylie Minogue | Malala Yousafzai | Stephen King | Napoleon Bonaparte | Galileo Galilei | Gabrielle Bernstein

Strengths and Inspiration | Part 2

Food for Thought and Action:

Is anyone born already being successful?

In a broad sense, no. We have to *do* something first in order to succeed—no matter what it is great or small, we have to act to make anything happen. We cannot just think about things.

No one is celebrated for simply being a prolific contemplater or dreamer. No way! It's what we *do* with our thoughts and ideas that matters. This includes: sharing ideas, activating others, collaborating, making things, building and co-creating, and adjusting our behaviors and activities.

Sure, successful people are often profound in their thoughts, dreams, and ideation—but it's the fact that they put effort behind them with *action* that separates them from the rest.

It might sound strange, but a good idea (all by itself) never did the world any good.

This doesn't mean that we must advertise our every great thought with the world; instead, a profound idea can change us from the inside out, it can revise the way that we see and interact with the world around us, which is a form of taking action.

So, again, what do all of these people have in common? It's not that they had great ideas. It's not their good luck. It's not their background. It's not their genetics. It's not their location or age. And, it's not mysterious.

Emily Dickinson | Rembrandt | Neil deGrasse Tyson | Christopher Soghoian | Picasso | Rob Dyrdek | Renoir | Penn Jillette | Mozart | Bach | Strauss | H.H. Munro | Voltaire, Dr. Seuss | Woody Harrelson | Shel Silverstein | Angie Vargas | Paulo Coelho | Jackie Robinson | Frida Kahlo | Spike Carlsen | Diams | Leonardo DiCaprio | Hugh Jackman | Neil Gaiman | Rosa Parks | Christian Rudder | Sally Mann | Georgia O'keefe | Louise Bourgeois | Edward Snowden | Toni Morrison | Jean Michel Basquiat | Andy Warhol | Lady Gaga | Alexander Calder | Jackson Pollock | Princess Diana | Nina Simone | Phil Anselmo | Prince | Bob Dylan | Venus Williams | Serena Williams | Gertrude Stein | Nikki Witt | Christopher Nolan | Spike Jonze | Rumi | Chris Rock | Sarah Silverman | Dwayne "the Rock" Johnson | George Takei | David Bowie | David Witt | Martha Graham | Walt Whitman | Bill Murray |Col. James Hecker | George Lucas | Paul Newman | Fred Rogers, Susan

Sontag | Simone Weil | Gaston Bachelard | Carl Jung | Bill W. | Joe Rogan | Greg Carlwood | Graham Hancock | Jack Welch | Napoleon Hill | Michael Jordan | Antoine de Saint Exuperie | Victor Hugo | Nikola Tesla | Arnold Schwarzenegger | Jeff Anderson | David Beckham | Jim Carrey | Jay Z | Robin Williams | Stephen Spielberg | Whoopi Goldberg | Chris Farley | Helen Keller | Simone de Beauvoir | Barack Obama | Johnny Depp | Chuck Norris | T. Harv Eker | Bruce Lee | Tony Robbins | Yvon Chouinard | Mark Twain | Vladimir Nabokov | Joni Mitchell | Chuck Berry | Julia Butterfly Hill | Ralph Nader | Winona LaDuke | Bono | Pete Seeger | Ellen Degeneres

Strengths and Adding Our Unique Value to the World | Part 1

As a culture it can seem that we are obsessed with the notion of *bigger is better*. At times, it's as if *more-more-more* is the only way to improve.

So much so that it may even seem like the only ways that we can even identify growth of any kind is by being louder, brighter, and more massive and extreme than before.

In doing so, we neglect the value added to our shared human experience by those who develop subtle virtues like: patience, open-mindedness, active listening, clear-sightedness, and balance.

Einstein said that *Everyone is a genius. But if you judge a fish by its ability to climb a tree, it will live its whole life believing that it is stupid.*

In that way, when we have a narrow definition of what growth can be, we put blinders on to the value that we add to the world. When we compare our unique value to someone else's— and leave no room for anything more—we risk comparing apples to oranges and fish to reptiles.

3 Questions

Looking back on the last 1000 days, how have I grown as a person? Be specific, name specific examples.

What makes me unique, what are my qualities?

How do I add my unique value to the world each day?

One Action

Spread Gratitude, Start a Domino Effect: Open your text messages and scroll down the the very bottom (aka Those whom you haven't messaged in a while). Pick 3 or four and send them the simplest message: "I am grateful for you." Or, if that feels too intense or out of character, try: "I was thinking of you, hope you are well."

Strengths and Adding Our Unique Value to the World | Part 2

Imagine how strange it would be if we devalued everything that we didn't have an *immediate* use for.

Say, for example, we are fixing a broken chair and need only a Philips-head screwdriver. We don't look at the flathead screwdriver and think, "This is absolutely useless."

Simply put, we know that it's not the right tool for the job—but it does have a purpose, given the right circumstances.

And, that's like us. We each add our specific value to the world in specific ways in specific situations. We won't be able to thrive in *every* condition, no way. We can, however, tune in and *learn* from every situation and grow in our understanding of others and ourselves in all that we do.

Sometimes adding our unique value to the world means getting out of the way and allowing others to shine where we may not be able to. This means that we no longer have to pretend that we can do everything and *be* everything. By slowing down and making room for others to add their unique value to the mix, we co-create environments where energy and ideas can be safely exchanged—environments where personal power is shared and where learning and teaching can be reciprocated.

3 Questions

What is one area of life or the world that I would like to know more about?

Who is someone in my life who knows more about this area than I do?

What is stopping me from connecting with them and asking them to share with me what they know?

One Action

Practice saying, "I don't know." It's simple, the next time you don't know something say, "I don't know". It may sound obvious, but try it, say, the next time that you are with a child who asks a lot of questions. Children are bound to ask things that we, adults, don't actually know—so, instead of approximating, changing the subject, or looking it up on your phone, just say, "I don't know." And then follow it up with, "What do you think? Let's imagine the possibilities together."

Strengths and Grit | Part 1

Grit.

Scholar and author, Angela Duckworth, defines grit as "a combination of passion and perseverance for a singularly important goal". She even invented the tool for measuring it: The Grit Scale.

So, what does this mean for us? Well, if we don't already possess it, we can be inspired by those who do, which is virtually everyone who has ever had a biography written about them—well-known examples include, J.K. Rowling, who was rejected by 12 publishers before finding a home for Harry Potter; and, Thomas Edison, with his 1000 failed attempts at the light bulb.

Better than being inspired, we can also *learn* from those who have grit and borrow their tactics. Duckworth observes that it's about more than just hard work, it's about developing a persistent belief in the vision and adapting ways of staying actively engaged in its pursuit, especially when the going gets tough.

This is to say that grit involves: hard work, persistence, belief, adaptability, action, and engagement (aka a focus on strengths). More than that, this success principle is based on an intersection of mind *and* body—one's ability to put in the hours physically *and* stay true to the focus.

It's important to acknowledge that grit is found first in the hands of an underdog: someone who has the odds against them, needs a miracle, or is laughed for their vision. After all, would there be any need for grit from someone who is not attempting the difficult, the impossible, the never-been-done-before, or the unknown?

*Think of that person in your life who is practicing grit and going against the odds and send them a little message today, let them know that you believe them.

3 Questions

What are my core beliefs?

Am I someone who sticks things out even when it's tough? Yes, no, sometimes, it depends?

Why do giraffes have purple tongues?

One Action

This is an action that strengthens the brain and improves your abilities to hold complex pictures in your mind—a skill that is handy for problem-solving and solution-creation. Add to that, it's fun. Here's how it works, find three photographs, postcards, or magazine images. Lay them out in front of you, one next to the other. Set the timer on your phone for 3 minutes. During this time, memorize the images, soak them in down to their last pixel. When the time goes off, reset it for another 3 minutes and sit back with your eyes closed. In that relaxed position try to recreate each image in your mind detail by detail. See and re-see everything in your mind. Do not open your eyes and peek until the timer goes off. Practice this daily for best results.

Strengths and Grit | Part 2

5 Thoughts

It takes more time and energy to create something than it does to destroy it. Plain and simple.

So, the creation of something as extraordinary as lasting change in our lives is going to be a process. And, because it doesn't happen overnight, as we progress incrementally, we have time to take in the scenery and overthink things.

That is, the road to shifting the paradigm is lined with reasons to quit, reasons to stay in our comfort zone, and reasons to do something else. It can be easy to get lost along the way or give up entirely. This is why staying focused on the *vision* is key, as opposed to the *outcome*. Focusing on the vision allows us to enjoy the ride, focusing on the outcome forces us to miss everything along the way. In that way, the quality of our grit is directly linked to the clarity of our vision.

Yes, it's true, grit can mean staying focused on a goal and putting in relentless effort to reach it— on the flipside, there is another type of grit, which might be known better as crippling fear or obstinate stubbornness, wherein a person remains steadfast and determined *not* to change.

In which case, the vision is one of despair and hopelessness, which, too, will come true when it is the center of one's focus. Grit bends both ways.

So, is it more effort, sometimes, to stay the same than it is to change?

3 Questions

When is a time that I persevered?

As a child, how did those around me show (or not show) grit in how they were living?

How far is up?

One Action

This is a thinking exercise that can produce really profound results in the realm of changing your mood. You can start this exercise feeling down in the dumps and walk away from it feeling renewed. It takes ten minutes and all you need is a pen, some paper, and your phone. Write down ten positive words in a list on the blank page— they don't have to be connected directly and they can be memories, too—anything that triggers feelings of joy.

For example:

Love
The cabin
Kittens
Summertime
Chocolate
Payday
My nieces
Poetry
Laughter

Set the timer on your phone for ten minutes and work your way down the list, thinking about each word for a full minute and then moving on. The energy that they create stacks on top of itself, line-by-line, and by the bottom it can feel almost euphoric to have spent ten minutes conjuring up the feelings of these words.

CONFIDENCE
COMES FROM
HOURS AND DAYS
AND WEEKS OF
CONSTANT WORK
AND DEDICATION.

ROGER STAUBACH

Strengths and Going Back to Basics | Part 1

Don't watch the clock; do what it does. Keep going.
Sam Levenson

Living from our strengths means recognizing who we are and then making conscious decisions to become more of that person.

Today is a day for action.

Whether we have a schedule or not, when we wake up in the morning, we do not know what all will happen in our day. After all, there are 7.5 billion other people running around on the planet—each with free will, just like us.

So, the question becomes: Do we *feel* free? Are we trying to be someone else? Are we trying to be something we are not?

If we are not becoming more of who we really are, who are we really becoming then? What exactly is holding us back from feeling a complete fullness of purpose in our lives?

What action can be taken in this exact moment to create a shift toward feeling fully present in this moment—do I need to make a call, send a text, set a boundary, pay a bill, schedule an appointment, meditate, or eat a meal?

Strengths and Going Back to Basics | Part 1

Today is a day for action. As are all days. And, in once sense, a decision itself is an action—but it's only one part of a whole, which involves a physical act or a change in behavior. Decisions are *mental actions*, and until we say something or do something, this process remains private and therefore only affects the person thinking it.

The decision itself is the inner component of the action—and, while essential to progress, decisions *alone* get nothing done in the real (shared) world.

So, if the start of change is, indeed, the result of decisions and actions over and over—it is then a *collaboration* of the inner and outer worlds, which are always affecting each other, that creates change. Our thoughts affect our actions, our actions produce results, the results affect our thinking. And around and around.

The art is this: How can the effects of their swirling interaction be consistently productive?

The answer is this: When it comes to goals, the best first step is to start small and be consistent. For example, the guy at the gym doesn't get ripped by going in and lifting heavy once...no. He gets ripped by going in day after day and making incremental gains. Make every action count.

BIG IDEAS

Making positive and lasting changes in our lives can sometimes seem like an overwhelming, complicated, or impossible task. At times, it might seem and feel like we are in a rut, spinning in circles, and that there is no clear way out. And, that might be true, in one sense—that is, that there is no *clear* way out—but, when we have had enough and are ready to take action, there is always a way out. That "way" is called: action.

That said, in order to take action, it is wise to consider our strengths, to be sure, and it is also wise to assess what *type* of action best suits the changes that we are trying to make. Change is not a one-size-fits-all proposition.

However, when it comes down to it, there are really only three *major* categories that lasting changes fall into. They can be considered in the following ways: The Tooth Brushing Type, The Haircut Type, and The Scar Type.

The Tooth Brushing Type: Consider this, if we want to have stronger and healthier teeth, we cannot just brush our teeth *really* well one day and then call it good for a while. No, in order to have lasting dental hygiene, we need to brush our teeth everyday. There is no easy way around that one—it's just the way it is. This is a daily maintenance action, and certain changes in our lives follow this same model. For example, if we want to grow stronger, we cannot just lift weights for 10 hours one day and expect results—instead, we need to take consistent action over the long term to realize our goal.

The Haircut Type: This is the type of change that requires periodic and specific attention—much like getting a haircut. Like The Tooth Brushing Type, we cannot just one day get a *really* short haircut and hope to never need one again. However, unlike The Tooth Brushing Type, we do NOT need to get a haircut each and everyday. So, for this type of change, we need to take a concentrated action every few weeks or months for it to be fixed and lasting. These types of actions are things like: regular visits to the chiropractor, naturalpath, or doctor; revising our budget; intermittent fasting; staying in touch with friends and developing relationships, taking vacations to recharge, getting massages, cleaning out the closet, and paying monthly bills. We don't need to do these things daily, but we *do* need to do them sometimes if we plan on thriving and staying on course.

The Scar Type: This is the type of change that most people, at some point or another, wish could be *all* changes. That is because The Scar Type is the action that amounts to this: Once and then done. It is an action that we take once and then move past it: it is permanent and it's not going anywhere. Changes that fall into this category include: choosing to exit/end a toxic relationship, quitting a habit once and for all, learning a new skill (like riding a bike, which you never forget), and paying off a debt. When it's done (and truly committed to with all of our heart) it's D.O.N.E. This type of change is the rarest because it requires what can be called "massive action". These changes are largely decisions, which tend to feel difficult, but that feel amazing when they are implemented. The Scar Type changes our lives in an instant—we go from living in one state to living in another state immediately and swiftly.

So, what type of change suits your needs, desire, and vision *right now* for the sort of shift that you are trying to make?

Strengths and How Change Occurs | Part 1

BIG IDEAS

Unusual as it may sound, change in the outerworld *begins* in the innerworld. That is, what we *think* about, we create.

Specifically, what we think about *most*, we find the most of in our lives. For example, if we begin constantly thinking about a certain type of car that we want, we suddenly see it on every street. Parents-to-be report seeing pregnant women "everywhere," when before it was only every once in a while. Or, if we think someone is irritated with us, we will find evidence of it in how they interact with us—even if they are *not* miffed in the slightest, we will still "find" it.

Where we focus our mental energy matters because our dominant focus tells our mind what to look for. In brief, what we focus on expands.

The thoughts that we think *repeatedly* condition us to expect, anticipate, and await certain events, scenarios, and exchanges. When we think a thought enough times, we naturally (and unconsciously) begin to look for it. After all, wouldn't it be odd if we heard the same message over and over and over again and remained totally uninfluenced by it? In this way, change occurs through *repetition* and our mind adjusts incrementally to accept certain things over time as normal and/or true. Think about fashion trends. At first, certain styles can seem absurd, but after months of seeing them everyday, they are just ordinary. We get used to things. We accept them. We stop paying attention. Our thoughts are like this.

So, how does this all relate to creating change? There is that saying, "If you do what you've always done, you'll get what you've always got." So, if our innerworld sculpts our outerworld by telling us what to look for; and, if our perceptions are crafted over time though repetition; if we want to change our lives, doesn't it make sense that we must first change what thoughts we repeatedly think?

Okay, sounds great. But, how do we *do* that? We do that in two ways. The first is by limiting what we actively and passively expose our minds to— garbage in garbage out...right? This includes other people, the news, social media, and entertainment. If it does not support the mindset that we are trying to cultivate, we must weed it out. (If it cannot be eliminated, we are wise to do what we can to at least be *aware* of it and limit our exposure to it.) The second way is to begin planting seeds-of-thought that we *desire* to be realities in our lives. These are affirmations. We can say, "I love feeling happy" and "I am grateful for all the joy in my life" even if we don't necessarily feel that way in the moment. And, through force of repetition, our mind will begin updating its "files" to notice more and more evidence that these ideas are true and all around us. Our positive attitude will begin attracting more positive people and experiences into our lives because we are training our mind to *notice* them.

If this is uncomfortable, start with something concrete. Try telling yourself, "There are tons of people with blonde hair in this town" and repeat it to yourself often. Inevitably, your attention will be drawn to each and every blonde person who passes by. In this case, your mind is not "creating" blonde-haired people, instead it is merely *noticing* what is always there. You can do this with anything.

Change can occur when we tell ourselves specifically what we want to change and then begin the process of cultivating our thoughts to create an awareness of its presence.

> IF YOU DON'T LIKE SOMETHING, CHANGE IT.
> IF YOU CAN'T CHANGE IT, CHANGE YOUR ATTITUDE.
>
> MAYA ANGELOU

Strengths and Water

Our strengths are always on. My acknowledging their presence, we allow ourselves to see the best versions of ourselves and others.

There is the story of two catfish—one old and wise, the other young. One day they are swimming along the bottom of a lake when the young fish says, "I heard the turtles talking about something called *water*, do you know what that is?" The older fish says, "Nope, never heard of it." And on they swim.

That's it. That's the story. What can be made of such a thing?

It's unlikely that the moral here is that these fish are simply dense and clueless. Instead, it probably points to something deeper—like the fact that the fish cannot see the one thing that is all around them.

It is literally their whole world and they have never experienced anything outside of it. Because they are so *completely* surrounded by water, it becomes impossible to perceive. In some ways it makes sense that, to a fish, water would be difficult to notice. It's like air to us. Which, of course, is the point.

The story is meant to teach us—humans—
something important about life and ourselves.

And, although the main *idea* centers around the
fish's narrow perspective, the main *message* isn't
saying, "Broaden your horizons, step outside your
comfort zone and live to a new extreme."

No.

Instead, the message, which is so much simpler
than that, it says, "Open your eyes." Asking, "Are
we truly aware of what is right in front of us?"

Perhaps it's a lesson in awareness. Perhaps it's
one in gratitude. Either way, it begs the question:
What is staring us right in the face?

We could start by looking around at the world.
Air. Lots of it. But what is it, really? How can
clear, empty space be described?

Or, light itself. Is it possible to bring our minds
into a state where we can marvel at something as
omnipresent as light? Light is all around us—lots
of different types, too, from natural to artificial to
colored. How could it all be explained? What
would it take to feel in awe of light?

What about blinking? We do that all day long.

When is the last time we cultivated an awareness of how important it is to blink? Or breathe? Or swallow?

No, it would not be practical to *always* occupy this state of awareness—but for a moment or two? Perhaps.

But, really, why bother thinking about this type of thing?

Because it's likely that we are missing out on something worth our attention. Our strengths, after all, function in this way—and our strengths are, when we allow them to be, the main drivers in our success and wellbeing.

Like water to a fish, they are so much a part of who we are, how we think, and the actions we take that it can be easy to fog them out and no longer see them. It can be easy to flip on autopilot and coast...

Being such a natural part of who we are, we may take our strengths for granted. However, because they are at the core of our greatness, when we lose sight of them, we lose sight of the best version of our self.

The same is true for others, for the people in our lives. How easy has it been in the past to take someone for granted? How quietly did it happen—as we lost that initial awareness and awe of their uniqueness? As we began to simply feel entitled to their gifts, qualities that were once so new in that first dawn of knowing them?

Uncomfortable as the thought may be, it seems improbable that we could make it to adulthood without experiencing this—from both sides. And, while it would be impractical to live in a *constant* state of awareness and praise, how important might it be, even after years, to reawaken that understanding of others' greatness. How vital might it be to remind someone—a fellow fish— that they are more than just the water we swim through each day?

Questions for Thought and Action:

Who are the most important people in your life?

How do you encourage them in their path and acknowledge their unique greatness?

What are some of the key ways you've been privileged to watch others grow and evolve?

How many different ways can you say, "I see you. I know you. I love you."?

Strengths and Not Overcomplicating Things

As we grow in our strengths, we feel more and more confident in our awareness that we are in the right place at the right time.

Known for his subtle but always innovative style, French composer Maurice Ravel described his own music as "complex but not complicated."

Because the words are so similar—and sometimes used interchangeably—his statement sounds a bit like a contradiction in terms. It could almost sound at first like he is saying "six of one, half-dozen of another". However, complexity and complicatedness are, in fact, vastly different ideas.

Nature, for example, is wildly *complex* in its ornate systems and flamboyant mysteries, which create and sustain life. We can all agree that it is certainly not simple.

But, can we really say that nature is *complicated*? Not really. That word, by definition, implies difficulty, strain, and, even, an element of the unnecessary. Anyone who has studied, or even sat in nature knows that there isn't really a "struggle" going on. Things happen as they must and that is that.

Sure, life at all times in the forests and oceans is vying for nutrients and space—but there is an ebb and flow to it. An order. There is an obvious cycle being enacted and reenacted.

Consider the activity of a wooded valley, there is no deliberation or hemming and hawing. Sun rises, sun sets. If a tree can't grow any longer, it dies and becomes fertilizer for the soil or home for insects and mushrooms. It is not moral or immoral, it isn't a place were "choices" are made by leaves and bushes. Things just *are.*

So, it may just be that things shift away from complexity and toward complicatedness only when we enter the equation.

As human beings, it begs the question, "What would it mean to live a life that is complex but not complicated?"

When we live in our strengths, we are likely to face complexity without complication. Complexity being, perhaps, challenges with a value, while complicatedness being the opposite. The strengths give us a knowledge and a language that serve to streamline our actions and weed out the unnecessary "noise". This allows us to tune into ideas that support the creation of the best versions of ourselves, while avoiding that which limits our greatness.

Through the strengths we don't have to wade through complicated mazes of self-doubt and perplexity. By developing a new mindset where we look for our others' qualities as well as our own we no longer question our motives and our path. We learn to accept and love ourselves for who we are, where we are. We have hope because we have a gameplan: a language to demystify our selves and others.

We can feel good about what we are doing and we can *allow* ourselves to feel fulfilled by our actions and decisions because, complex as they may be, we know they are leading somewhere.

Questions for Thought and Action:

Are you pursuing your own dreams or someone else's?

What about your life is beautiful *and* complex?

What about your life is complicated?

What would it take to shift the balance from complicatedness to complexity?

Are you working toward your own greatness or someone else's?

Strengths and Perpetual Growth

Because we are always changing, we are never done knowing ourselves. The wisdom of the strengths remains true as we evolve.

There are more than seven billion of us on the planet right now. And, at this moment, we are each of us thinking, dreaming, wondering, or imagining something. We are vast. And, similar as we might appear at times, no two of us are the same. We all have skills. We can all bring something to the table.

With that in mind, what can be said to be the first ever skill mastered by a human being? It probably wasn't juggling or ventriloquism. It was likely the development of an ability that sustained life, right?

Humans, for example, mastered fishing more than 42,000 years ago. Not "got good" at it. Not "figured it out". But, *mastered* it.

Researchers found the remains of thousands of ancient fish in an Australian cave. And, not just any old bones, either—amid the piles were those of tuna, which, even by today's standards is a difficult catch. That is to say, our ancestors weren't just dropping a line in the water and hoping to get lucky. They had clearly figured out something that worked and they used it to their advantage.

So, if fishing was *mastered* more than four millennia ago, how long did it take us to realize that we could even fish in the first place? After that, how many years did it take for us to get good at it? And what was that process like? When it comes down to it, we've probably been *trying* to catch things in the water forever...

Fast forward to the present. Despite everything else that is happening in our world—including Twitter and bacon ice cream and competitive horse jumping—people still, to this day, go fishing. Add to that the fact that it has evolved into a more than $130 billion industry worldwide and we can glimpse both the spectrum and the existential magnitude of human capability.

Now, let's consider the opah, which was discovered for the first time this year. Put aside the fact that it is huge, bright orange, and shaped like Frisbee, it is the only truly warm-blooded fish.

Wait, what?

We've been masters at hooking, netting, trapping, spearing, scaling, cooking, and eating fish for more than four thousand years and we are *still* finding new ones? Not only that, but species of fish that break the mold on what we thought about them in the first place? (i.e. cold-blooded and all)

Though, when it comes down to it, it really isn't that surprising. In fact, it's likely that we will be pulling new and exotic life forms from the ocean forever. Which, when we allow it, is like the process of learning, knowing, and discovering ourselves. We continue to do it all of our lives.

Whether we are skimming the surface or dredging the depths, aren't we always learning new things about who we are, were, and can be?

The strengths provide a steady guide in this adventure because even as *we* change, they stay the same. The actual words and ideas, that is, are static—our abilities to interpret their wisdom grows and evolves as we do.

Think of when we re-read a book and get something totally new out of the second time through? Don't we ask, " How could I have not seen that the first time?" After all, the sentence themselves didn't change between readings...*we* changed.

And, so it is with our strengths. The more we think about them, the more their depth is revealed. Choosing to think about our greatness and seeking to develop it can reveal an entire matrix of options and opportunities. It can mean the difference between dropping a single line into a pond (normal life) and casting a vast net into the sea (strengths life).

Because, as we change, our abilities to incorporate, understand, and apply more and more complex ideas into our lives is heightened. From there, we can begin to encourage a strengths perspective in situations that before would have baffled us.

In that way, like the early fisher-people, who probably practiced for centuries through trial and error, we, too, have the opportunity (and the *honor*) to practice being and finding new layers of ourselves.

The strengths, as always, give us starting points and steady ideas to return to.

Questions for Thought and Action:

So, in what ways are you perpetually growing?

What would a list of your greatness consist of?

What are some step you could take toward deepening your understanding of yourself?

How could you cultivate a greater awareness?

Or, a few moments of conscious reflection before bed?

What questions can you ask of your life—and could the strengths be the answer to some of them?

Strengths and Avoiding the Comparison Trap

When we allow our strengths to work together we uncover the unique value of our wholeness.

Consider the complexity of the human body and its systems. Imagine every organ performing its special function and notice how each one does what it is designed to do. Like gears in a watch, each part both supports *and* relies on the next, and together life is maintained in the body. It wouldn't matter if there were twenty healthy livers, if the body lacked lungs—or vice versa. Each individual piece plays a role that is absolutely essential to the whole.

That said, wouldn't it be strange if the heart grew jealous of the pancreas for being able to produce insulin—or if the kidneys became distracted and envious of the stomach for its capacity to digest food?

The absurdity of this might not be all that different from when we compare ourselves to others and feel less-than as a result. The strengths tell us that there is only one thing worth focusing on: strengths. Achiever is no better or worse than context or positivity or input. Just as the lungs aren't better than the gallbladder or the esophagus or the brain.

Einstein said it best: Everybody is a genius. But if you judge a fish by its ability to climb a tree, it will live its whole life believing that it is stupid.

In that way, a person with, say, ideation is likely to feel frustrated if they measure their worth by how capable they are of executing specific, concrete tasks. After all, how can we fault an orange for not tasting like an apple?

Living in our strengths does not mean being good at everything. Nor does it mean being able to do what someone else can do. Instead, it means knowing who we are and taking action to become more and more of that. We develop most in our strengths. Period.

In addition to that, developing a strengths *perspective* means being able to see greatness in others and appreciating it—even praising it—as opposed to feeling threatened or less-than by it.

Questions for Thought and Action:

What does your greatness look like in the mirror?

Who can you begin to honor as opposed to envy?

What would it take to grow more aware of the

unique value that *you* bring into the world—
gratitude list, conversations, vision statements,
deep breathing?

Strengths and Puppies

We are always changing and growing, the strengths provide a toolset that allows us to get specific in the ways we track our evolution.

Most of us can agree on one thing: puppies are the cutest.

And, if we've ever been with someone in the first days of their new pet we know how genuine happiness looks. The carefree energy of the young animal somehow draws us into a place of peace and joy. It's their defense mechanism. It's nice to be around. As babies, we too, held the same tactic.

Now, let's imagine that we go out of town for a while and return to find, not a puppy, but a dog. To us, it might not even seem like the same animal, while to the owner it might not seem like the dog has grown at all.

This is called the "puppy effect". It's what happens when we witness gradual changes over time such that we don't really notice them.

And, it's perhaps easiest to experience this phenomenon within our own self. After all, we spend all of our time being ourselves, so much so that it is easy to overlook change as it happens incrementally. In some ways this is natural, in other ways it may allow for some of our greatest achievements to fade into the background.

Without a language to articulate our unique greatnesses, it is difficult to truly benchmark our individual successes and growth. Without a system to track and measure our development we are likely to sell ourselves short. Luckily, the strengths provide us with a vocabulary that makes the amorphous tangible and the abstract specific.

With that in mind, it may become important to not only *think* about our strengths, but to actually keep record of when, where, why, and how they are playing a role in our lives.

The simplest way of doing this is by setting aside a few moments each day for reflection. Taking two minutes—that's right *two* minuets—to jot down a few thoughts about the development of our strengths perspective provides a record that we can later look back on. It creates concrete reference points that we can compare our current thought-process to that of days gone by.

Questions for Thought and Action:

Without a journal of this type, are you able to see and track your growth and development?

What are other ways and methods that you could use to benchmark your greatness?

Is it important for all of us to even be keeping tabs on such evolutions?

Is this something that keeps you in the moment, out of the moment, little bit of both, neither, depends on the day, depends on the person?

YOU CAN'T CROSS THE SEA MERELY BY STANDING AND STARING AT THE WATER.

RABINDRANATH TAGORE

Strengths and Being Ourselves

The strengths help us get specific about who we are and how we can bring out our real selves with others.

Oscar Wilde said it best, "Be yourself, everyone else is taken."

So, why can that seem so daunting?

Perceptions. Realities. Expectations. Fear. Too many options. Too few options. Pressure. Distraction. Negative self-talk. To name a few.

If we are human, we know what it is like to *try* to live up to the expectations of others.

Many among us were brought up believing that we would be accepted if only we acted a certain way, or if we followed a set of rules, listened to this or that music, earned a specific amount of money, or reacted to life in a prescribed way.

Reality is, if we feel that we cannot be ourselves, how is it that we reason that we can be someone *else*?

In some ways that seems infinitely harder, no? In other ways it feels like a safer bet, because if we are rejected for being someone else—well, it's not *really* us who is being rejected...

In that way, being ourselves requires vulnerability. That is the baseline. So, it might be essential to remember that we *all* have specific qualities that add value to the world and that we are all in the same position.

Before the strengths we may have had hunches about what this meant, but no real language for expressing it. We may have thought, "I am good at meeting people." Or, "I like helping others." Or, "I am confidant only in certain situations."

While such an awareness is a *start*, it certainly is not a roadmap. Liking to help others is a bit vague, right? There is, of course, a solution for that.

The strengths provide us with a vocabulary that illuminates the difficult-to-describe qualities of ourselves. It's a language that does something important right away: It puts a specific name around an abstract concept of our personality. Then, it articulates general traits about us that include actions and/or places to look for action.

After all, it isn't enough to be told that we are "always curious" about something. That isn't very useful. Instead, if we are made aware of our strengths of input, learner, and/or ideation, for example, we can begin to frame our thinking around concrete concepts in a language shared by others.

Once we can do that we can begin to share our self-discovery with others. We might do this actively (Saying, "Guess what I learned about myself?!") or passively (living by example)— either way, when we are open to being who we are, we are able to find identification with others.

More than that, when we develop a pattern of looking for strengths in others, we begin to develop a high-quality mindset—one that looks for solutions instead of problems, one that finds things to like about others as opposed to dislike. It's a mindset that *expects* good things.

From there we discover that if everyone else has strengths that benefit us all, we must have them too.

Questions for Thought and Action:

What would it take to shift to a perspective where you focused on everyone's awesomenesses; one where you walked into situations saying, "I wonder how So-and-so is going to impress me today?" Or, "I wonder what new thing I will like about them?"

What would it look like to truly be yourself 24/7?

Whose voice echoes in your ears telling you who you"should" be?

Does the opinion and judgment of that person really matter? Why or why not?

Strengths and Thinking, Part One

Our thoughts and views are affected and fed by outside forces. The strengths provide productive and instructive food for thought.

Conventional wisdom would tell us that all thoughts come from one place: our brains.

If that is so, how did they get there in the first place? After all, we are not born with all of our thoughts pre-formed. Each morning our brains don't select a folder with that day's thoughts in it. No way. Fact is, we really have no clue what thoughts we will have as we roll out of bed.

We gather ideas, beliefs, interests, judgments, opinions, and views moment by moment—the whole time getting input from outside sources.

We develop our mindsets by living, observing, feeling, and interacting with others as well as our environments. Day by day we construct and cultivate the *type* of thoughts we have based on the *types* of situations we create and experience.

The people we spend time with, the places we go, the books we read, the sites we visit, and the shows we watch actually craft our worldview. Each one encourages a certain type of thinking.

Each one promotes a specific idea about the world around us.

What we expose our minds to has an effect on how we perceive the world around us.

An easy way to see this is when people say, "I don't watch horror movies because I don't want to be scared all the time." Whether a person sees a movie or not does not change the world itself—however, it *does* change the way that that person sees the world. The ideas from the film (outside) are carried with them (inside) and affect their thoughts elsewhere in the future.

We are constantly in this process.

Big picture. Let's consider the current impression that we hold of ourselves. Whatever that may be, we were not born thinking that. In fact, as babies we didn't even know that we were a "self". We just *were*.

Life, through our experiences, conditions our self-image. Many of the thoughts we have are social and cultural constructs, ideas that literally start outside of us...and then work their way in.

So, if the outside affects the inside, isn't it worth considering who and what we are subjecting our brains to?

The strengths give us a consistent language to tap into, one which describes the world and others in ways that are productive, generous, and solution-minded.

The strengths give us something valuable to focus on. When they become our dominant thoughts, we have created a strengths mindset. And when we have that, we have powerful glasses to view the world through.

The more we tune our inner-language to a language of strengths, the more we attract meaningful situations and interactions. Why? Because we begin to *look* for strengths and share them. This doesn't mean that everything has to be roses. No. Instead we develop an awareness that we can grow from our interrelations with the world around us—that life can be a process of building up as opposed to breaking down.

Questions for Thought and Action:

What have you been feeding your brain with?

Who has been teaching you how to think and react?

Who have you been teaching to think and react?

How often do you thank your true teachers in life?

How do you define the term "teacher"?

Strengths and Thinking, Part Two

Our strengths, like our thoughts, are nourished by different sources. When we know what to look for we can find fuel for our minds, bodies, and spirits. The strengths provide a looking glass.

Let's start this out with the same question from last time...

Where do thoughts come from? For real, where is it?

Conventional wisdom would tell us that all thoughts come from one place: our brains.

Fact is, biologically speaking, this has become a dated idea. The science and medical communities have determined that there are *two other* hubs of neural activity in our bodies: the heart and the gut.

There's even a new division of medicine known as neurocardiology, which studies the heart as a thought center and a generator of consciousness. Wired with more than 40,000 neurons—which are cells that carry messages— the heart communicates with the brain. These heart cells can sense, feel, learn and remember and, literally, affect the brain's processes.

Not only that, one in three cells in the gut are these neurons. We've all heard the expressions "listening to our gut" and "butterflies in our stomach", well, it turns out, that these are actual results of neurological activity in those areas. Ideas are literally being created and processed in the gut and then sent up to the head for evaluation. That's why it can feel so strange to "have a hunch".

If all this was not enough, heart transplant patients routinely report having new memories after the surgery, which later prove to be accurate to their donor's lives. In some cases, recipients are capable of performing new skills that their donor's knew—composing poetry, playing the piano, and solving mathematical equations.

Thoughts are happening all over the body and then channeled to the brain for review—which makes sense, since the brain has the *most* computing power, weighing in at more than 100 billion neurons.

That said, we all know those who lead primarily with their heart, gut, or head.

Our strengths are no different. That is, the strengths are the places from which we lead. They are our foundations. And our strengths create meaning in our *lives* in the way that the body's neurons create thoughts in our *minds*. Our strengths transmit messages to us about how to live.

We are all fueled by different sources and our greatness manifests in different ways, but at the end of the day, the result is the same: action. Like thoughts through a brain, our strengths channel themselves though our lives, experiences, and activities. And, when we allow them, they reveal to us the path of highest value to us.

We all know that learning is good for the brain—well, action is good for our strengths. It's not enough to simply *know* our strengths, we have to *do* things with them. And, this doesn't mean that we have to take run a marathon, or buy stocks, or propose to our sweetheart today. Instead, strengths-guided action means that do something that moves us toward our greatness.

The strengths encourage us to take action—we might get this as a hunch (gut) or as a thought (brain) or as a feeling (heart)—and when we listen, we find that we are always being guided.

Questions for Thought and Action:

How do your strengths communicate with you?

What does greatness look like today in your life?

What action can you take today that moves you in the direction of your dream life or a life goal?

Did you have any goals when you woke up this morning?

What would change if you sought out new fuels for your strengths?—people, places, things, YouTube videos, music, books, websites...

Strengths and Immeasurability

We have infinite potential and because we can never outgrow our strengths they build on one another and evolve with us forever.

Look up.

The sun is 92.96 million miles from us right now. That's the same distance as running 3,548,092 marathons. Seems like a pretty long way away, right?

Now, get this: That is relatively close. Scientists have measured light that has been traveling at 200,000 miles per second for 10 billion years.

It's almost incomprehensible how far away that is.

And still, wherever *that* is, it isn't the furthest place in the universe. Not even close. In fact, there is an unknowably larger distance beyond that. And beyond that distance, another one and then another one.

Some describe the universe as being infinite—and they mean it literally—as in *limitless.*

The beauty of our strengths is that they, too, are without bounds and inexhaustible. Imagine the thought of someone saying, "I've mastered belief. So much so, in fact, that I no longer have any use for it." Or, "I've used up all my empathy. Fresh out. Guess I'll have to find some other way to view the world..."

No way.

Reality is actually the opposite of this scenario. That is, the more we *use* and *apply* our strengths, the more they grow and the more we receive. Imagine a pencil that gets longer the more we write with it. That's the strengths.

What a gift!

They are not like a bucket of paint where the more we use the less we have. No. In fact, we *have to* use our strengths to keep them!

Our strengths are like candles, which can light millions of other candles without dimming as they share their light.

Questions for Thought and Action:

How is it that you gain more strength by using it?

What else is like that in your life, in the world, or in nature?

What does greatness look like in your life today?

Was it the same yesterday?

How have you been evolving?

Has it been in drips, in cascades, or somewhere in between?

Strengths and Focusing

What we emphasize in our thinking, we find more of in the world. When we emphasize strengths, we find ourselves surrounded by them.

It's very simple. What we think most about, we find more of in the world.

We've all likely had the experience where we notice a sound—a dripping faucet, a ticking clock, someone who scrapes their fork when they eat—and after a point it becomes the only noise we hear. Our minds hone in and focus on that sound until it gains all of our attention and drowns out everything else.

The same dynamic is present in our global perceptions, too. That is, the big ideas that we live by are really just the select few that we've chosen to focus on (out of the billions out there). Our values. Our beliefs. Our philosophies. We cannot ascribe to everything, so, at some point we decide what stays and what goes–and the ideas that we keep become the basis of our worldview. They become the foundation of our reality.

In other words, we train our minds to locate and perceive specific things by thinking along certain lines. That which we consider to be relevant to our lives, interests, and well being, we detect. Almost everything else we either gloss over, block out, or ignore.

Imagine, for example, what a vegan and a meat-lover would notice in a brand new grocery store. They would certainly hone-in on different products. Because they have unlike needs they do not perceive the same things—even though they are in the *same* place, doing the same thing: grocery shopping.

What we deem important, we find because we look for it. And, it is worthwhile to remember that we don't all believe that the *same* things are important. So, in that way, we are all noticing and remembering different and various details.

Reality is based on our past experiences, present knowledge, desires, and fears as well as our perceptions. The fact that two people are in the same *space* does not mean that they are having the same *experience*.

Another easy way to see this is by observing an over-protective parent around their child. Say, for example, that they are walking though a forest on a path. To the child, the world is virtually one big playground and danger-free–tree to climb, berries to eat, things to pick up and throw. To the parent it is fraught with danger and risk–places to trip and fall, poisonous plants, deadly insects.

In reality, it's neither *and* both.

Because, reality, in this case, is about what is anticipated—for the child it is *fun*; for the adult it is *safety*. And, so, the child looks for fun and finds it, and the parent looks for safety and finds it.

The strengths give us specific ideas to frame our thoughts around–they give us a litany of things to anticipate. They give us concrete words to look for and...*find*. Not just in our own lives, but in the world and in the lives of others.

If we try to live outside of our strengths, we are likely trying to find what we are not best equipped to see. It's like reversing the roles of the parent/child in the forest—can we imagine the child trying to be over-protective of the parent? And the parent on a mad-quest for fun?

Probably not. The child and parent are wired to seek and find their appropriate realities.

By honing in on our strengths and the language of strengths, we can maximize our chances of finding realities that push us into greater and greater potentials.

Questions for Thought and Action:

What are you looking for in the world?

What is your dominant thought process?

How are *you* wired?

What is your natural course of action in situations?

How often are you tuning into yourself or to the voices of others?

About the Author

Zach Carlsen is a writer, coach, and artist. His strengths of *Ideation, Connectedness, Input, Strategic, and Empathy* have taken him all over the world. He is an inventor, athlete, joyous wanderer/wonderer, translator, poet, & Gallup Certified Strengths Coach.

Find more at ZachCarlsen.com

Made in United States
North Haven, CT
22 June 2023

38088694R00096